If I Could Be A Doughnut

If I Could Be A Doughnut

Peter A. Letendre

iUniverse, Inc.
New York Bloomington Shanghai

If I Could Be A Doughnut

Copyright © 2008 by Peter A. Letendre

iUniverse books may be ordered through booksellers or by contacting:

iUniverse
1663 Liberty Drive
Bloomington, IN 47403
www.iuniverse.com
1-800-Authors (1-800-288-4677)

Because of the dynamic nature of the Internet, any Web addresses or links contained in this book may have changed since publication and may no longer be valid.

The views expressed in this work are solely those of the author and do not necessarily reflect the views of the publisher, and the publisher hereby disclaims any responsibility for them.

Illustrations Copyright © Marci McAdam

ISBN: 978-0-595-50022-2 (pbk)
ISBN: 978-0-595-50309-4 (cloth)
ISBN: 978-0-595-61345-8 (ebk)

Printed in the United States of America

This book is for my wife Patricia, whose love and support are with me always. I would also like to thank my dear friend Marilyn McNally, who gave positive feedback throughout.

Dedicated to the memory of my grandmother, Ethel Valentine Smee, a grand lady who loved unconditionally.

Contents

Preface

I wrote this book to amuse myself while enduring a long episode of flu. After the flu left, I was still writing. It seemed that I got a bug of a different sort. I enjoyed stepping into a world where animals, insects, dreams, ghosts and strange monsters gathered and mingled with kids and cowboys to make life a little lighter.

The poems are meant to celebrate what it means to be a child. The book's title poem, "If I Could Be a Doughnut," captures the unifying concept behind all of the verses—a child's imagination is a priceless joy to be celebrated. I hope that we never lose that magic, no matter what our age.

If I Could Be A Doughnut

Angel Earthling

Here he comes, the angel-faced little boy,
sneaking around the house with his new toy,
a space gun, the kind that makes a clatter,
forcing nervous hearts to flitter-flatter.

At imagined aliens, he takes aim
and startles the curled up cat. Like a flame
it rockets up a wall and clings for life
on the ceiling, breathless, stiff as a knife.

Now to the kitchen with his ray gun gleaming,
where Mama's drying dishes, daydreaming.
He just sees a clone wearing frockery.
One loud zap and there goes the crockery.

Deep asleep, old Grampa's a pile of bones,
he splutters, twitches, snores and somehow moans.
In the boy's eyes Grampa is cosmic crust
who, without warning, he lasers to dust.

Now in his room, his toy taken away,
this tiny, dreamy-eyed earthling gives sway
to being a pirate on the high seas,
and writes to Santa, "Next year, a sword please."

Ballad of Bullfrog Phil

In marshy ponds where tadpoles flow,
and scented lilies boundless grow,
the bloated bullfrogs swallow flies
then croak the song of warty guys,
a rhythmic count of throaty beats
with dungeon tones that oft defeat
the younger frogs, whose voices crack
and warble notes like mallard's quack.

Among this group is Bullfrog Phil,
who startles all with voice so shrill
it conjures up a shrieking ghoul.
So off he's sent to froggy school
to learn the art of ribbet tones
that rumble deep and vibrate bones,
but Phil, whose piercing, wailing screech,
finds plunging scales beyond his reach.

He fails at school and leaves disgraced;
back home he's mocked for lacking taste
and moves to fields across the way—
too close for comfort some would say—
to spend his days without his kin
consuming flies or sleeping in.
Content to live in lazy cheer,
he sings away throughout the year.

One night a grizzly bear arrives
to devour lots of bullfrog lives
but Phil, alert, blasts out a blare
of chilling screams that leaves the bear
bewildered. Fearful, it retreats
and tries another source of eats.
The grateful frogs name Phil as king,
and pass a law to let him sing.

Barn Dance

Keep the beat by clicking spoons
to country fiddlers and their tunes.
Jump and holler, clap your hands,
make a clatter with old tin pans.
Feel the rattle in your bones
from tapping toes on cobblestones.

Jigs and reels drive you crazy;
catch the fever, don't be lazy.
Dance on tables, dance on walls,
Dance on stairways or down the halls.
Infectious strains take you high.
Don't let this moment pass you by.

If I Were a Boat

If I were a boat with nowhere to be,
I would simply float like waves on the sea
to somewhere remote and completely free.

Campground

A blush of colour
washes clean upon a lake
dirty with acid.

Rusting under smooth wet elms,
barrels of malignant chemicals
sit as happy as campers.

Granny

Without sentiment or grace
the tapestry of time unfolds upon her face,
revealing delicate art
as natural to the heart
as sun-washed golden leaves
or roses in a field paled by morning vapours.

Tiny Lost Fly

A tiny lost fly
arrives in Kauai
and beaches at old Poipu.
With little to do,
he waits in the sand
to tickle the toes,
perhaps the nose,
of people like me and you.

Grapes in a Cluster

Grapes in a cluster,
with juicy luster,
beg me to take a taste.

Squirty and fruity,
totally hooty,
not one is left to waste.

Butterfly

A nomad from the sky
with iridescent wings,
flutters across my palm
like a rainbow in flight.

It frolics merrily,
with gentle floating dance,
before slipping away
in a winking whisper.

Bogeyman

Moving silently through silky shadows,
like a spider on feathery tiptoes,
the bogeyman from lairs of darkness crawls,
avoiding light, slithering when it falls.

Wild are its eyes, alive with trickery,
its mouth contorts, fiendish with snickery,
as it hides in your room somewhere, scheming,
but light a lamp and it departs, screaming.

Ziggy, the Penguin

Ziggy, a penguin from icy South Pole
waddles along on his twice daily stroll.
He's of the Emperor species, you know,
tuxedo clad with cheeks of orange glow.
At four feet and ninety pounds, he's no slouch
and he's a sweet-natured thing, not a grouch,
yet this bird refuses to explain why
he swims like a torpedo but can't fly.
He'll sleighride on his belly down a hill,
careful not to stumble or take a spill
to join his mate and his furry chics, too
and play hockey with the South Polar Blue.

Ghost Town

Dusty, drained of colour and dry as bones,
a sad, abandoned hamlet squeaks and moans
and arranges itself like graveyard stones.

This place was built with intentions to last
but a run of bad luck ruined things fast:
when the mine bottomed out, the die was cast.

The town that remains will never console
the secrets forever locked in its soul,
a sorrow that aches while tumbleweeds roll.

Doughnut Milk

I dunk a doughnut in my milk,
which is cold, bubbly, smooth as silk.
Soon the dough becomes soggy slush,
and falls away in blobs of mush.
My glass now swims with sloppy bread,
a concoction I drink with dread.
You see, doughnut lumps make me sneeze
and tickle my throat until I wheeze.
I set the glass aside and smile
and munch a brownie for awhile.

Marquee Value

Imagine a chipmunk named Leaf,
whose name gave him endless grief.
He changed it to Chippy,
but friends thought that dippy,
so he blew them away with Sharif.

Hiccups

I have hiccups
with minds of their own.
Sometimes they're silent,
but often they moan.

I also burp
an echoing boom,
that scares the hiccups
right out of the room.

Classroom Diners

Kids find strange things to eat in class
from eraser ends to pencil points,
inky pen nibs and chalk.
They even gnaw the cork off the back of rulers
and lick gobs of paste.

All this makes me wonder
what do they eat at home?

Cabin Fever

When the cold winds blow amid pine and snow
I burrow in my lodge like a beaver,
consuming the days in dull, wasted ways
like a sad, pathetic, self-deceiver.
From week to week, I grow weary and bleak
with the telltale signs of cabin fever.
Empty and glum, I turn loony and numb
and start swinging at ghosts with a cleaver.
From the rafters I shout, raving no doubt,
like a frothy, wild-eyed true believer.
Then up pops a voice, with words ripe and choice,
and the gruffness of a lifelong griever.
Oh how he drones, melting marrow in bones,
fetching slights and woes like a retriever.
Finally I say, get lost, go away,
but it's me I'm talking to, by Jeever.

First Snow

The dead burnt autumn surrenders to flurries in the night,
a bluish-white carpet of snow, lumpy, crunchy and new,
twinkles like sugary crystals under the pale moonlight,
then turns to a tinseled glaze with the morning's icy dew.

In a snowdrift someone's bike lies on its side, out of sight,
along with an old leather boot owned by goodness knows who.
Soon bundled young tots dance through the snow and shriek with delight,
before hurling big, fat snowballs yelling, "This one's for you!"

The Crocodile Who Ate Himself

With stealth and guile, the crocodile
glides by a mirror in the swamp.
After awhile, he spies a smile
showing a wicked, snarly chomp.

In waters dim, the Croc is grim
when encountering things that dare
to mimic him with taunting whim,
or meet his icy, warning glare.

His eyes flash bright, so full of fight,
and his wide jaws could snap a tree.
With one quick bite, I'll put things right
he says licking his chops with glee.

To his dismay, his sneering prey
crumbles in a mouthful of glass.
Winning the day, he slides away
convinced his opponent lacked class.

Dust Bunny

A fuzzy dust bunny,
odd shaped, rather funny,
with three fingers, two toes,
and clad in snazzy clothes,
saunters across the floor
with attitude galore.

Then it glides through the air
natty, suave, debonair,
and floats down to the street,
where a parade of feet
unwittingly provide
a sort of carriage ride.

Clinging to a big shoe,
and a pant leg or two,
it tours the sights and spies
a house, just the right size,
and scoots under a bed
beside a dog named Fred.

Shirt Brat

You said that my shirt was older than dirt
and blamed the poor cat for dragging it in.
Right, like the cat is a collector, babe.

You said it was rank, which meant that it stank
with the foul odors of ancient road kill.
So the smells are truly historic, babe.

You said it was sad, quite horribly bad,
that I wore a shirt that moved on its own.
I like the term radioactive, babe.

You said it was white and totally bright
after you washed the daylights out of it.
It's no longer a conversation piece, babe.

"Billy, stop calling me 'babe'!"
"Okay, Mom. Sorry."
To myself I said, "You've trashed my shirt, babe."

Guitar Player

Cowboys and drifters and no account dudes
shadow the bar like a pack of bad moods
soothed by the play of an outlaw's guitar
who, like an angel, plucks strings from a star—
soft, gentle strains of an old lullaby
that touches them deeply, none knowing why.

The clattering flutter of bat wing doors
reveals a wrangler out to settle scores
with that lowdown scalawag, Johnny Mean.
Boys at the bar back away from the scene.

But outlaw Johnny continues strumming,
and in the silkiest tones, starts humming
the haunting refrains of old lullabies
that ease the hardness in the stranger's eyes.

He falters, stares, not knowing what to think.
No longer itching to create a stink,
he slumps in a chair unable to gauge
how a simple tune could undo his rage.

Meanwhile, the dim saloon stirs back to life,
a live or die tension no longer rife,
as hands and drifters return to the bar
to listen to the outlaw play guitar—
soft, gentle strains of an old lullaby
that touches them deeply, none knowing why.

Garden Wonders

When young and crawling on my knees,
amid the flowers big as trees,
I wonder if I'll grow so high
to see the petals eye to eye.

Among the scented blooms, I see
a caterpillar big as me
then spy a little butterfly
shivering, delicate and shy.

When a shower suddenly springs,
wetting a leaf where an ant clings,
I run indoors, get warm and dry
and hide from thunder rumbling by.

Dancing Lion

In Africa's sandy Kalahari,
there is a playful young cub named Larry,
born with the gift of dancing in his soul.
Lyric rhythms shadow his every stroll,
and soon he's leaping as easy as pie,
touching the treetops or clouds in the sky.
How lively he steps in a graceful way,
gliding on hind legs in a jungle ballet.

Jiving along to a rapturous beat,
Larry ignores the movement of his feet,
and the hidden mesh net he's dancing on.
The melodic drums, hypnotically drawn
are the lure, the enchanting lullaby
to snare the sweet, beguiled passerby
amid the windswept grasslands. When ropes snap,
a tangled rush of tough cord seals the trap.

Aboard a ship, Larry's stuck in a hole,
a dark, cramped place that would drain any soul,
and taken overseas to someplace cold,
a jewelled urban jungle, blaring, bold.
Restrained in a cage behind heavy bars,
no longer able to dance beneath stars,
Larry despairs at life's lack of reward,
until he sees a kid on a skateboard.

The child spins in a clatter and loops the loop.
Larry copies, and jumps a pretend hoop.
A gathering crowd demands an encore,
hoping the lion will do a lot more.
Some play bongos to give Larry the chance
to release his jungle spirit and dance.
He tumbles and glides with effortless pace,
born of freedom, unrestricted by space.

House Guest

Surveyor Sam's old hut was occupied
by a small furry beast with lots of pride.
Sam wondered how best to get the thing out.
He yelled but it ignored his every shout,
so he poked and jabbed a stick in the door
but it was snapped off and eaten. What's more,
most of Sam's gear was scattered on the grass.
This critter had attitude, if not sass!

Sam was annoyed. He missed his cozy shack
and would do all he could to get it back.
Bent on a showdown, or an all-out war,
Sam brought in a specialist, a wild boar,
who strained on a leash and grunted with glee,
eager to crush the beast or make him flee.
What followed was a blast of snorts and moans,
as the boar was tossed back, a pile of bones.

Sam burned some wet leaves making thick, black smoke,
convinced the dogged brute would run or choke,
but the cantankerous creature held fast,
and Sam, now rattled, wondered who would last.
At wits' end, he eyed stacks of dynamite,
and with a mighty boom, they did ignite,
leaving no trace of Sam's shack with the blast,
though the stubborn intruder left at last.

Aardvark's Banquet

Tony Aardvark, whose long nose slants
along the ground searching for ants,
figures there's an easier way
to unearth his lunch every day.

You might think Tony's a dreamer,
or just an old fashioned schemer
who thinks the food in the region
would lure the ants by the legion.

He spoons out some sugar at will
on places where there's an ant hill,
and when the ants march out in file
Tony's ready to dine in style.

The Dinosaur and the Toad

Gronking, groaning, making an awful shout,
Dawn, the dinosaur, thumps and bumps about.
She has a high neck, a bulky round jaw,
and a whimsical face that shines with awe.
Her wide, gentle eyes are sleepy and pale
and match the grey of her long bumpy tail.

When Dawn thunders along eager to play,
smaller critters panic and run away,
frightened by her size and her noisy romps,
or how she trembles the earth when she stomps.
This baby dinosaur, far from full grown,
will learn from elders to be on her own.

One day, while out playing, she finds a toad
pinned by his shirttails 'neath a rocky load.
He shivers in fear as she pulls him free
and begs, "Oh please dinosaur, don't eat me."
She feels so bad for his outburst of fears
that her eyes well up with a rush of tears.

"I couldn't and wouldn't do that to you,"
she says, letting out a loud sniff or two.
After talking, they smile and start to play,
becoming happy friends along the way.
And now they stick together, side by side,
an odd pair hopping along, stride for stride.

Johnny Sandals

Among the leather-faced, range-tough cowpokes
Johnny Sandals is one of those odd folks
who prefers Buddhist verse and tarot roots
and beat up sandals over cowboy boots.
He's a quiet lad without any guile,
happy in his thoughts, always with a smile.

He can ride and tame any beast alive,
from bulls to outlaw ponies, and survive
to read about the stars and shoot the breeze
or sing to the sunset, strange melodies
from the Far East; tones that trigger a howl
from packs of moon sick wolves out on the prowl.

He says he's at peace with the universe,
leaving some cowboys to shrug or disperse
at such a vast, overwhelming notion
of a wave contented with the ocean.
All they know is, despite his spaced-out joy,
Johnny Sandals is one solid cowboy.

Canadian Coins

Maple Leaf pennies are copper and bright,
with millionaire tastes and budgets too tight,
while fluttering sails of the Bluenose dime
linger timeless like a mariner's rhyme.

On quarters, the stalwart Caribou waits
with majestic bearing that captivates,
while Beavers work away on the nickel,
building their dams that leak not a trickle.

A lonely Loon haunts a wilderness lake,
a scene replayed with each loonie we take,
while a Polar Bear strolls across the ice
and brings in a toonie for twice the price.

Now loonie and toonie rarely agree,
but there's one small point they share to a tee.
These former members of the paper cash,
deeply resent slumming with coinage trash.

Hockey Goalies

Busy hockey goalies,
padded from head to toe,
with sticks and mitts
and sprawling splits,
eat pucks as much as snow.

On cold, arena ice
spectators roar and frown;
no time to think,
or even blink,
with forwards bearing down.

So it goes, end to end,
with action, thrilling thoughts.
But in the net,
there's one sure bet,
the goalie must stop shots.

Flight of Fancy

Let's take a flight of fancy,
said the hippo to the flea,
and float on marshmallow clouds,
lighter than snowflakes can be.

Let's loop the custard pudding,
said the bug-eyed little flea,
and nibble crispy wafers
nestled on the ice cream sea.
When with a clang, school bells rang;
the flea trudged off in sorrow.
Worry not, the hippo said,
we'll fly again tomorrow.

Ghoul's Soup

While prodding through the gurgling slop,
fat steamy bubbles flip and plop
and choke my breath with such a bite
that I see stars, like sparks of light
reflecting bits of greasy mould
rank as toe jam or fish too old.

Curly noodles slither like snakes
'round chunks of floating wormy cakes
and great green gobs of gooey waste
clogged with toenails for extra taste.
I'll spoon it up and slosh it back
until my innards melt and crack.

Home Repairs

Our tap broke so Mama called the plumber,
who came promptly with his tool kit,
but he broke his finger trying to unscrew the tap.
He had to go to the hospital.

Mama called for another plumber.
This one didn't know beans about taps.
He fiddled with them, pulling one thing, then another.
When we tried to get water, the lights went on.

Mama, still cool, called for another plumber.
This one yanked everything out then took a break.
He never came back. They say he went to Venezuela.

Getting a little irate, Mama called yet another plumber.
This dude drilled holes in the ceiling,
installed a jet fan, built a huge fountain in the living room,
and made our garage door dance.

Mama put her foot down. Enough was enough.
She wanted someone to fix this tap once and for all.
Another plumber came and undid all the damage
and, in the process, our house collapsed,
so we decided to move to a shack in the woods.
The water runs freely there.

Jam-Faced Maggot

The jam-faced maggot wiggles and dangles
and sloths along at ponderous angles,
thriving in darkness, unseen in clutter,
it oozes forward like melting butter,
licking its chops for the thrill that awaits
from eating fried chicken right off the plates,
or fresh apple pies with cinnamon cream
or marshmallow tarts that taste like a dream.

This tiny blob slithers from room to room,
drawn by aromas that linger and bloom
from tangy slops of marmalade jelly
or other sweets that tickle its belly.
When it finds a tin of blueberry jam,
it drools and gobbles it down, gram by gram,
then waddles away exhausted, well fed,
and scrounges the trash in search of a bed.

Grumbling Onion

An onion grumbles to a carrot, I really don't like peas,
and zero is my tolerance for tomatoes if you please;
nor have I the stomach for zucchinis, yellow beans or beets,
and I can't stand green spinach, turnips, or cauliflower treats.
I'm a lousy veggie traitor, so says purple aubergine
to squads of leeks and mushrooms, led by lippy lima bean.
Broccoli and cabbage understand me; so, too, do the sprouts.
As for celery, cucumbers and parsnips, I have my doubts
unless they're all mixed together in the most delightful way,
to make a spicy meat pie, served piping hot in pots of clay.

Master of the Universe

Winter moved in like a shivering ghost
and I, in my cabin, had to play host
to crazy ideas that filled me with woe,
like could fire freeze at forty below?

The pain of the winds echoed all around,
relentless as wails from dogs in a pound,
forcing me to cover my ears and weep
for five straight days without any sleep.

I paced in a daze, right out of my head,
half of me alive, the other half dead.
Along the way the fire faded, then died,
and frigid winter's bite staggered inside.

Thinking I was done for, I rested my eyes,
then heard a tribal voice, awesome and wise.
Saved in the nick of time, I said, amused,
as that voice spoke again, this time enthused.

Okay, Yukon Trapper, come in and eat.
We've stacks of pancakes and a special treat.
I shot from the tent like a cannon ball,
my feet barely touching the grass at all.

Later in bed, I muttered with a smile,
tomorrow I'll be on a South Sea isle.
How I love this world of pretend, I said,
and pulled all the blankets over my head.

Kangaroo Lou

In from the Outback, it's Kangaroo Lou,
hopping bow-legged, looking wistful, too,
as he bounces along jangling his spurs
like a saddle tramp all tangled with burs.

He arrives in town with fire in his eyes,
determined to win the big dancing prize.
No chance, folks say, he's a one time wonder,
a simple drifter from way Down Under.

Inside the dance hall, the band is playing,
and dancers in turn are flying, swaying
to toe tapping tunes well loved by the ear,
receiving whoops, hollers and bursts of cheer.

Next on the dance floor is Kangaroo Lou,
leaping high and wide like a buckaroo,
flawless, dashing, no hint of a blunder,
he slashes through air like silent thunder.

The crowd rises in a sea of applause,
demanding encores with boisterous hoorahs,
which roll like a wave, a hypnotic trance,
stirring Lou to give an amazing dance.

And when he's done, the ballroom falls quiet,
then erupts into a full blown riot.
Now we all know that Lou's still a wonder,
an awesome legend from way Down Under.

Hallowe'en Jazz

Round midnight on Hallowe'en,
Duke Skeleton cooled the scene,
playing jazz at goblin's crypt.
Everyone who heard him flipped.

Tickling the ivories he crooned,
while bass and percussion swooned,
and gremlins swayed entranced.
Even Jack-O-Lanterns danced.

Ghouls, with accordion bones,
rattled time to fluid tones
as Duke burbled silky scat
like a smooth, hypnotic cat.

Then, at the approach of dawn,
like a phantom he was gone.

Little Amanda

Little Amanda is a bear,
who moves around from here to there,
searching the woods for yummy treats
like baskets filled with picnic eats.

She leaps about on fluffy paws,
climbing the trees with pointy claws,
then lounges in the shade awhile
while all the leaves rustle a smile.

Amanda's a cub, not yet grown,
and doesn't wander far from home.
Mama's nearby, alert, aware,
quick to protect her darling bear.

Little Fishes

Everybody wishes
the frisky little fishes,
swimming unsuspicious,
will nibble on their hook.

Refusing to be dishes,
no matter how delicious,
the saucy little fishes
prove smarter than they look.

If I Could Be a Doughnut

If I could be a doughnut
from the inside looking out,
I would say the hole in me
is a part that I left out.

I could fill the space, I guess,
with ice cream, syrup and jam,
but who needs a sloppy mess
when I'm fine the way I am.

Mutant Toe

I have the oddest foot you know,
it's saddled with a mutant toe
that thinks itself a buffalo.

As it wiggles it seems to grow
and tower over my big toe
making it wince aloud, "Oh no!"

Can mutant toes be friend or foe?
Opinions range from high to low.
It's part of me, that's all I know.

Snail Blues

Lumpy McDumpy is one sorry snail,
clumsy and awkward in every detail,
made all the worse by the shell that he lugs,
something not shared by his cousins, the slugs.

He's frumpy, slumpy and dislikes his looks,
and is often reading those self-help books.
Now, as he stumbles and bumbles along,
he pours all his feelings into a song.

Like a stuffed sausage, I just crawl around
sliding on mucus over the ground.
Who can love me? I'm a big horrid slob
with two long antennas and a hard shell blob.

If I were lucky, and who's to say not,
I could be a charmer, a real hotshot,
or better yet, by an old apple tree,
find Molly Mollusk just waiting for me.

Paulie, the Rain Drop

Sitting forlorn in the fluffy clouds, young Paulie is stewing
as orders say he can't do what other raindrops are doing.
He's too slow, too small and a risky thing to ever let fall.
He needs more work, say the brass, if he wants to make it at all.

"I'll make it," Paulie asserts. "You just wait and see."

So this tough little raindrop is drilled and put through his paces
till he's good to go in the armada of rainy faces.
He splashes down to earth, sliding along a wide, leafy stalk,
then joins a growing puddle in the middle of a sidewalk.

"Okay," he says. "Next time I'll kiss the flowers. Just wait and see."

Old Delaware

With acrobatic flair
a portly circus bear
called old Delaware
did handstands on my chair.

"Hey, listen Delaware,"
I said, "You take care!
You could fall from there."
He didn't seem to care.

"Why don't you play elsewhere?"
I said, with little fanfare.
He gave me a frosty stare
that seemed to say, "Beware!"

Then I remembered ...
he's just a teddy bear.

Lobos

They prowl ancestral trails
with cold, fierce eyes,
mavericks gnawing on the food chain
amid timber, snow and rock.

Endangered, their packs thinning,
they defy the injustice
of shrinking territory
and the encroaching stealth of man.

Haunted by mystical stirrings
as deep as space,
they howl a desolate song
to a black sky, a white moon.

Trails

Lying under an endless, starlit sky,
hearing crickets, owls and a wolf's sad cry,
a cowpoke from his bedroll is stirring
as flames 'neath a coffee pot are purring.

A passenger jet enormous in scale
soars overhead, leaving a lonesome trail
in its wake, a long stream that seems to stay
and blend into the sunrise faraway.

As cowboys break on a high, quiet bluff,
moving their cattle along in the rough,
they sense the romance of the western range
is a way of life that will never change.

Oxford Blues

Two soulful, Oxford heels,
each with ten tiny eyes
and rather high arches,
peevishly and rudely,
poke their tongues out at me.

I've earned their displeasure
for leaving them unlaced,
scuffed and unpolished,
and going on a walk
with those breezy sandals.

Maxie

Maxie's an elephant, sweet-natured, wise,
with thick ivory tusks, enormous in size.
His big, swaying trunk—a very long nose—
blows like a trumpet and curls like a hose.

If you look closely, guess what you'll see?
Maxie's got eyelashes like you and me.
He's big and slow like the rest of his herd,
but if he stampedes the jungles are stirred.

A bulky bull with a belly that sags,
and wide, floppy ears that flutter like flags,
yet despite his size he's a peaceful sight
but, if threatened, he'll charge, ready to fight.

Maestro's Orchestra

The instruments start with bellicose roar,
first one, then another, then dozens more,
tubas, pianos, trumpets and trombones
elbow the clarinets and saxophones,
then cellos, flutes, violins and oboes
scuffle with bassoons, harps and piccolos,
followed by the thump of big, bass drums,
as triangles, cymbals, chimes and snare drums
eye the xylophones and glockenspiels,
while the English and French horns act like heels.
Above it all, with a wand for a whip,
is a wild, long-haired geezer, sort of hip,
called the maestro, the master of the band,
who brings order with a wave of his hand.

Whiff of Lonesome

Lonesome's a drover from old Abilene,
who herded spooked steers and rarely stayed clean.
One day his horse pitched him, gave him the snub,
"Whoa!" it snorted. "You best bathe and scrub."

So Lonesome soaped up and washed himself blue
lathering honeysuckle through and through.
Back on the trail his pardners grew wordy.
Lonesome just smelled a trifle too purdy.

Chez Pup

Dressed in a tuxedo that barely fit,
a short-haired mutt with a shiny bald head
waltzed through a French cafe like he owned it.
The others stared but not a word was said.

He was the maitre d' of the old Chez Pup,
and fed the palates of the finest hounds.
Dumpy but jolly, he would guide their sup
with a special service that knew no bounds.

His waiters would swarm like bees from the nest,
bringing juicy meats with a barking snap.
When hounds licked their chops in a howling fest,
he'd keep them in line with a tactful yap.

Santa Anxieties

On a cold Christmas Eve, with snow piled high
and blizzard winds howling a lonesome cry,
I nestle in bed with a worried face,
wondering if Santa will find our place.
I grow hushed, tense, straining every which way,
to hear the jingle of reindeer and sleigh
but the only sound is a passing train
blowing its whistle in mournful refrain.

I lie here yawning, unable to sleep,
excited by the endless thoughts I keep
like imagining what's in Santa's head
when he tastes spicy taco gingerbread.
Will he think I'm nuts for leaving a note
asking if he prefers milk from a goat
or something more bubbly with lots more cheer
like a huge mug of old fashioned root beer?

I wonder on this and a whole lot more.
Will he choose the chimney or use the door?
Should someone warn him about the loose rug,
how it rolls up and traps you like a bug?
Then there's the matter of our tricky tree.
"Don't even breathe on it," Dad said to me.
"If it falls like the walls of Jericho,
tinsel, ornaments, everything will go."

How will Santa get around in the dark?
Using lights will make the neighbor's dog bark.
He'll no doubt meet Python, our rascal cat
who, if he's stepped on, will knock Santa flat.
Does he ever miss someone on his list?
If so, does a do-over chance exist?
From all my worries, my mind is weary.
I hope I don't always think this dreary.

On the Good Ship

Lollipop Cow
managed somehow
to sail the open sea.
She picked a boat
that kept afloat
and drifted far and free.

Carried along
by tide and song
and stars of fixed degree,
she reached the shores
of old Azores
and caused a stir, you see.

Glowing reports
from nearby ports,
brought her celebrity.
Now Lollipop Cow
gets mobbed, and how,
by folks like you and me.

Outlaw Genie

I came upon a copper pot
and banged it with a spoon.
I must have hit a magic spot
while clanging out a tune,
for all at once a phantom came
as haunting as the moon.
This ghost, who like a cowboy spoke,
was howling out his name.

"Howdy. I'm Durango Mayhem,
a mangy genie dude,
who loves to take things and break 'em.
I'm rotten, mean and rude."
With that, he snatched my magic pot—
the man was truly crude—
and with a simple twisting stroke
produced a well-tied knot.

I stared, my mouth agape.
He snickered, haughtily and weird.
"Man, you're in real bad shape,"
he said, scratching his scraggly beard,
then added, "Gotta fade."
As for wishes, he had, as feared,
long mastered the cruel joke:
"Sorry pardner, they've been mislaid."

And then with a poof he was gone
and I, rather annoyed, moved on.

Soap Eater

My brother, the dope,
ate a chunk of soap.
More than a nibble,
more than a bite,
but less than a whole bar.

He did it on a dare,
which began his troubles.
Now here's the scoop.
When he tries to poop,
it comes out like bubbles.

Queen of the Beach

Oiled in lotions, wearing shades trimmed in peach,
it's the Lady Bug, the Queen of the Beach,
who lies on soft blankets, sipping mint tea
enthralled by the sight of the deep, blue sea.

She lolls around like a summer bubble
drifting on inner waves, free of trouble,
and wiggles her toes in the cool wet sand,
while bathing in solar rays, getting tanned.

When it gets too hot, then off she dashes,
kicking full stride through the waves, and splashes,
encircled by a swirling foamy rinse
that is so shivering it makes her wince.

Back on the beach, drying in a towel,
she giggles and shrieks and lets out a howl,
eager to take a dip over again,
not just once or twice, but well over ten.

Now Lady Bug heads home to the city,
far from this shoreline romp, such a pity.
Maybe next time she'll convince the spider
to tag along and sunbathe beside her.

Immortal Prospector

Pappy McFarlane, a grizzled old fox,
lived by himself in a windowless box,
a ramshackle hut without any floor
and a squeaky, wheezy, lop-sided door.

Life was secluded, rigorous, remote,
the only way back was by Leap Year boat,
but deep in his heart, a hunger took hold
to be out in the hills prospecting gold.

High in the mountains, he toiled away
paying no heed to the darkening day,
when out of nowhere, a thick, foggy mist
brought bone chilling winds that hit like a fist.

Slipping and sliding the length of the slope,
gliding round curves like a wet bar of soap,
over he went off a sheer, snowy pass
into the depths of a yawning crevasse.

Ninety years on, with the gold rush a bust,
and Pappy's old lean-to a pile of dust,
an earthquake hit, and the force of its blast
restored missing pieces from ages past.

Among the debris now strewn on the ground
were cuckoo clocks with their strange little sound,
along with snowshoes and tins of brown beans,
and an ancient pair of Levi blue jeans.

And perched on the limb of an old oak tree,
an amazing vision for all to see,
the frozen corpse of mother lode Pappy,
clutching nuggets, looking fresh and happy.

The Wuggle

Here comes the Wuggle
lumbering to his feast
on five legs: a strange beast
with wide flaring nostrils
and a low slung brow.

This big, shapeless blob,
actually a slob,
has neither ears nor toes.
He had a finger once,
but where it went, no one knows.

Now here's the jive,
if he gets close,
really, really close,
he'll eat you alive.

Walls of Jericho

Jericho McDuffy,
a lippy young toughie,
fumed in his tiny nook.
"I'm a hard-nosed roughie
who rejects things stuffy
like reading that dumb book."

The teacher smiled sweetly,
while saying discreetly,
"Are you afraid to look?"
Outfoxed completely,
he surrendered neatly
as love of reading took.

Rabbit in the Hat

With long floppy ears, a twitchy pink nose,
and lumbering feet with wide, springy toes,
Jack is a rabbit who waits in a hat
reeking of carrots and acting the brat.

Dressed to the nines in a bow tie and tux,
his cottontail wags at life so deluxe,
but when magicians grab hold of his ears,
the rabbit's the stooge to bring on the cheers.

Weird Beard

When I get old I'll grow a beard
that's scraggly, itchy, grey and weird.
I'll let it grow ten years or more
and have it dragging on the floor,
concealing biscuits, jam and bread,
drops of egg and a bug that's dead.
If I'm lucky my beard will grow
and wrap this planet in a bow,
or tie itself to Mercury,
but that would be the end of me.
Such a thought doesn't leave me cheered,
so maybe I'll forego the beard.

Sebastian and Tom

Sebastian the Snail,
is perched on a pail,
watching the world go by.

Whatever passes,
slow as molasses,
he notes with careful eye.

There's Tom the sly cat,
a slow, skulking brat,
who thinks of snails as pie.

Outstretching his paws
and razor sharp claws,
old Tom swipes wide and high.

The pail overturns,
and the poor cat learns
his prey has wiggled by.

Sebastian, meanwhile,
departs with a smile
to safer worlds nearby.

Yukon Cactus

Don't know who planted it, or even when,
but Yukon's got cactus trimming the glen.
Seems the landscape—rocky, barren and cold—
has met its match in a weed, centuries old.

Will cacti survive the sub-polar frost?
Will the terrain give in, admit it's lost?
Will there be an ox for each side to gore?
Who knows? Tensions fill the air. We have war!

"Cacti are doomed," environment screams
to the thick, spiny shrubs used to extremes.
"We will snow you under! We'll freeze your roots!"
But cacti remain and flourish like beauts.

The weather now employs some nasty tricks:
eighty below blizzards with hail like bricks.
The cacti shrink in a survival crouch,
uttering not a word, not even an ouch.

Finally, with the buds of Spring, a truce—
then Peace—as things makes sense and have a use,
which explains the Midnight Sun fiestas
and the charming, winter long siestas.

The Cowboy Troll

Fiddles cavort in a frolicking trance,
as the boys from the trail await their chance
to ask a gal if she would care to dance.

Hiding in corners is Hickory Mole,
a stumpy, lumpy mischievous troll
who lets the music enchant his soul.

Grotesque, misshapen, at least at first glance,
this impish creature knows that in romance
his warm, fragile heart doesn't stand a chance.

Yet look closer, see behind his sad eyes;
see the hurts from those too quick to despise;
see the gentleness he can't disguise.

Which is why gals love him, try as he might
to avoid being hurt with bursts of spite,
and, when kissed, he shrieks away in wild flight.

Everyone stops, stares, astonished, tongue-tied,
as this excited dude scampers outside
where a rambling buckboard flattens his hide.

Sweet ladies help him to his feet and pinch
themselves at what they see. They blink and wince:
he's now a flawless, dime-a-dozen prince!

Darlings Who Have Gone

Lonesome cowboys in smoky bars
carry torches that light the stars
and flame a hurting song,
a melody of unhealed scars
that breaks the strings on old guitars
for darlings who have gone.

Hippo Hop

There's nothing more preposterous
than a hopping hippopotamus
who wiggles and shakes,
whatever it takes,
to mount a bike like the rest of us.

Lullaby

What dreams and golden scenes will be my last
of all the thoughts I keep?
Will I see boulevards or old bazaars,
or lions lie with sheep,
or slip away and tango with the stars
when time has emptied out the best of me
and filled me full of sleep?

978-0-595-50309-4
0-595-50309-8

Printed in the United States
120585LV00004B/28-30/P

9 780595 503094